Original title:
The House I Built

Copyright © 2025 Creative Arts Management OÜ
All rights reserved.

Author: Giselle Montgomery
ISBN HARDBACK: 978-1-80587-135-4
ISBN PAPERBACK: 978-1-80587-605-2

## **Threads of Continuity**

I raised the walls with mismatched bricks,
Each one a surprise, it's full of tricks.
The door squeaks loud, a comical sound,
A comedy stage in my goofy playground.

The roof, oh dear, it leans to one side,
Like an old hat, worn with pride.
Windows that rattle, they dance in the breeze,
A jigsaw puzzle that aims to please.

My floors creak tales of laughter and fun,
Every step's a giggle, each day's a run.
The kitchen's a circus, pots start to sing,
As veggies do pirouettes, a colorful fling.

So here I reside in this whimsical place,
Where chaos and joy have made their grace.
With threads of continuity woven in light,
Life's silly moments make everything right.

## Foundations of Memory

In the basement, my dog hid,
His conspiracies, quite absurd.
A treasure map under the lid,
For candy bars, we'd never heard.

Grandma's chair is quite the throne,
Squeaky sounds are her voice.
I sit down, feel right at home,
And she'll grumble, I've no choice.

## Walls That Whisper

These walls can hold a secret tight,
Like where we hid from Mom's loud calls.
They scheme and giggle in the night,
When we built a fort with old, stacked walls.

Giggles echo where friends have stood,
They share the tales of all our tricks.
The paint peels off, yet all seems good,
History lives, in the creaks and kicks.

## Dreams Framed in Wood

Laughter framed alongside the beams,
A swing's creak, brings joy anew.
Daydreams hang like crazy themes,
All captured in a frame or two.

Treehouses built with hope and glee,
No safety nets, just chilled spills.
Jumping high, we could not foresee,
The laughter that stems from those thrills.

## **Echoes of Childhood**

In the yard, a world to roam,
With sticks as swords, we'd battle foes.
A cardboard box can feel like home,
And superpowers, no one knows.

Hide and seek, we'd scurry around,
Hiding behind every nook and cranny.
Echoes laugh without a sound,
In this world, I felt quite zany.

## Stairways to Awareness

I climbed the stairs, what a sight!
Each step creaked, a gentle fright.
My cat soared past, in a sprint,
Thought I was late for a tea event!

The railing shook, held by a dream,
I pondered life in the beam of a gleam.
Fell for a shadow, I tripped with grace,
Landed right there, a soft cheek embrace.

## The Pulse of Place

In the corner, a chair made of fluff,
Each cushion whispers, "I've had enough!"
It laughs with me when I eat cake,
And judges me when I have a mistake.

The walls display my greatest mess,
From paint spills to weirdness, I confess.
Yet each crack and mark has a tale to share,
Of late-night snacks and daring repairs.

**Footprints in the Dust**

Oh, the dust bunnies are quite the crew,
Holding meetings where they plot and brew.
Each footprint tells a story untold,
Of mischief and laughter, both brave and bold.

I sweep them away, but they come back more,
Like old friends returning to the door.
In this grand space, we dance in delight,
Leaving footprints of joy, oh what a sight!

## The Audacity of Architecture

This structure's quite quirky, don't you agree?
With walls that lean, as if in glee.
The roof was a hat, a real fashion tease,
Waving to clouds with the greatest of ease.

A door that squeaks like a rusty tune,
It often debates with the light of the moon.
With windows that wink and say, 'Come on in!'
In this playful space, the fun will begin.

## The Portrait of Place

In my backyard stands a quirky shed,
With a family of squirrels that makes my bed.
The door creaks open, quite a loud groan,
It's the tiny home for a gnome I've outgrown.

A rickety fence sways at the breeze,
It holds back my dog who's prowling for cheese.
The flowers are all weeds in a colorful mess,
Yet somehow, I feel like I'm living in bliss!

## **Layers of Love**

A sticky note here, a souvenir there,
Each corner whispers tales of love and care.
The fridge is adorned with artwork galore,
To some, it's a mess, but to me, it's a score!

The couch is lumpy, a comfort zone churned,
With snacks still hiding where my dog learned.
Each layer of clutter holds a memory sweet,
Like the time I tripped over the cat's tiny feet.

**Foundations of Memory**

The kitchen's a riot with pots and some pans,
Cooking up meals with quirky plans.
I burnt the toast once, and smoke filled the air,
Now we toast marshmallows when friends come to share.

The living room echoes with laughter and cheer,
With mismatched furniture that we hold dear.
Each bruise of a bump has a story to tell,
About clumsy ballet in our own little shell.

## **Walls of Whispered Dreams**

The wallpaper's peeling, a sight to behold,
Covered with doodles, both wild and bold.
In corners, I stash all my secret bills,
A treasure map drawn with some minor skills.

The ceiling is low, so I duck and I weave,
Hoping the spiders don't gang up and grieve.
Yet each little cranny is filled with a scheme,
In the place I've created, I'm living the dream.

## **Labyrinth of Legacies**

My walls speak secrets, quite absurd,
A sock in the corner, nothing unheard.
Grandma's old cat claimed the throne,
While the dishes conspired to feel alone.

Pizza boxes stacked, like a sweet Jenga game,
Each slice a testament to my shame.
The vacuum, it roars, in a battle of dust,
In this maze of memories, I'm lost but must.

## Anchors of Affection

My fridge holds magnets from places afar,
One from a beach, one from a car.
They wiggle, they jostle, in lines, they stand,
Like my friends at a party, they just can't plan.

The couch, a maestro of my lazy tunes,
Comfy enough for naps or afternoon cartoons.
There's a blanket fort, my royal retreat,
With legos as guards, and imaginary sweets.

## Whispers in the Attic

Up in the attic, the cluttered parade,
Old trunks and treasures, a lived-in charade.
Ghosts of my childhood, they giggle and squeak,
As I rummage through boxes, all dusty and meek.

There's a costume from Halloween, a knight with a grin,
My sister's pink tutu, how did that get in?
A collection of trophies, well, half of a score,
Middle school victories, I still want more.

## Fleeting Footfalls

In each little corner, mischief is bred,
A tap-dance of dust bunnies, joyfully fled.
The floor creaks poems when I tiptoe past,
Like an old friend reminding me, nothing lasts.

My shoes play hide and seek every afternoon,
Dodging my feet like they're dancing to a tune.
With every footfall, a story is spun,
Of laughter and chaos, of two left feet fun.

## **Cornerstones of Belonging**

In the corner, there's a cat,
Who thinks he's wearing a top hat.
The furniture's had quite a chat,
Asking, 'Whose home is this? It's so flat.'

The plants have started a book club,
Debating over a sturdy grub.
Each petal dreams of a big tub,
While the couch just sighs, saying, 'Rub-a-dub.'

The fridge sings old rock 'n' roll,
While the dishes hide in a close shoal.
Stir-fry dances like a disco pole,
In this home where laughter's on patrol.

So raise a toast with milk and bread,
To memories living in every thread.
With crumbs and giggles as our spread,
We'll build this joy, though it won't spread.

## **Rooms of Reflection**

In the bathroom, a mirror does gloat,
Reflecting faces that play and float.
Shampoos whisper jokes, quite remote,
While rubber ducks form a quirky boat.

The kitchen's in chaos, pots on parade,
Spaghetti noodles in a wild cascade.
The chef can't recall how soufflés are made,
As the oven grins, 'Please, don't invade!'

In a bedroom that dreams of a pillow fight,
The blankets laugh out loud every night.
While socks wander off with glimmering light,
Creating mischief till morning is bright.

A closet sings with clothes piled high,
The shoes conspire to grab the sky.
In rooms like these, you'll never cry,
Just laugh until you say goodbye.

## Pathways to Tomorrow

Each step I take, the floorboards creak,
The path ahead is surely unique.
My shoes are squeaky, quite mystique,
Leading me on, a playful tweak.

Outside, the garden's in a dance,
With daisies prancing, taking a chance.
The bugs are buzzing, lost in a trance,
And ants do chacha, given a glance.

Sidewalks twist like a modern art,
Each crack a story, a daring part.
With bikes and scooters, we speed and dart,
Creating paths that warm the heart.

Tomorrow's door is painted bright,
With colors that sparkle in joyous light.
Each journey forward fuels the sight,
In this playful maze, all feels right.

## Shadows of Quiet Hope

In the evening, shadows start to sway,
A cozy corner where dreamers play.
Each wall listens to what we say,
With whispers echoing hopes on display.

A chair tells tales of days gone by,
Of laughter, tears, and a cat's sly eye.
It rocks gently as if to fly,
In the dim light where secrets lie.

The floor holds echoes of running feet,
Memories trapped in rhythm, so sweet.
Even the broom dances to the beat,
While dust motes spiral in lazy retreat.

So here we sit, as the day ends,
With a cup of tea and our closest friends.
In shadows bright with love that extends,
The quiet hope of tomorrow transcends.

## Landscapes of Love

In the backyard, a garden's sprout,
We planted seeds, just to see 'em pout.
With weeds that dance in the summer sun,
I whispered, "Hey plant, let's have some fun!"

The roof's a hat, tilted at an angle,
I swear it winks like a whimsical dangle.
Windows that smile when storms arrive,
Shouting, "We're safe; let's jive and thrive!"

## **Heartbeats in Hallways**

Echoes bounce off the walls so bare,
With my cat's paws, we kick up the air.
Socks on the floor, a colorful scene,
They dance like twirls of a silly routine.

In the hallway, I trip on a shoe,
It giggled and said, "You thought you knew?"
Laughter echoes from room to room,
While dust bunnies plot their next grand bloom.

**The Essence of Embodiment**

Chairs with stories of people past,
They creak and moan, but don't move fast.
A table that wobbles and tells a joke,
"Careful, or risk a dinner soak!"

Cushions that laugh when you sit too high,
They squish and pop, as if to sigh.
A fridge that hums a tuneful ditty,
"Snack time's here, oh isn't it gritty?"

**Resilient Reflections**

Mirrors that giggle when I pass by,
"That outfit's wild! You know you can try!"
Walls that whisper secrets of days gone,
"Remember that time you'd sing till dawn?"

Floors that squeak with a curious tone,
"Dance like nobody's home — you're not alone!"
With each goofy step, up and down I prance,
The rhythm of life is a playful dance.

## Framing Each Moment

I raised the walls with laughter loud,
As nails flew by, I felt quite proud.
My blueprint was a scribbled mess,
Yet here I stand, in sheer success.

The windows wink at all who pass,
With curtains made from old bedazzled glass.
I'll paint it bright with colors wild,
Come see my charming misfit child.

**The Space Between Moments**

In hallways where the echoes play,
Wander memories like kids at play.
My ceiling's low, my heart is high,
I duck to dodge the dreams that fly.

There's a closet where the socks conspire,
To hide away, like bold new liars.
Each corner holds a funny tale,
Of tripping on a rubber snail.

## **Memories Anchored in Place**

My kitchen's filled with leftover dreams,
Cereal boxes bursting at the seams.
A fridge that hums a silly tune,
And all my friends are spoons and forks in bloom.

I painted chairs a neon hue,
They're screaming, 'Come and sit with me too!'
Should you find crumbs upon the floor,
Just know they danced then left for more.

**The Breath of Brick and Mortar**

Brick by brick, I built my style,
Each day's a new, imperfect trial.
The roof's a patchwork of my woes,
Like an artist's canvas, it forever grows.

Pipes that creak like laughter light,
In shadows dance, my dreams take flight.
Every crack has stories sung,
In this funny fort where joy is flung.

## **Nooks of Neglected Dreams**

In corners where socks argue and fight,
A cat claims the couch in the morning light.
Dust bunnies dance, a quirky parade,
Echoes of childhood, like lemonade.

Old toys conspire beneath the bed,
A kingdom of fluff, where no one's bred.
Lurking in shadows, the remote lies still,
As I trip on a shoe—what a comedic thrill!

The fridge hums a tune, a not-so-sweet song,
Its shelves a buffet: both right and wrong.
Leftovers whisper of meals past glory,
Yet every bite tastes like an old, sad story.

Windows that giggle when the wind blows past,
Frame scenes of life, moving slow, moving fast.
Here in this chaos, absurd and profound,
Every odd nook holds a belly laugh sound.

## Seasons of Shelter

Spring brings the pollen, a sneeze and a giggle,
The door swings wide, with a proverbial wiggle.
A misplaced umbrella blooms like a flower,
As raindrops play drums for the foolish and sour.

Summer invites in the sun's fierce embrace,
But the A/C cries out—can't keep up the pace!
Sweaty and smiling, I lounge on the floor,
Living room weekends, who could ask for more?

Fall sweeps in leaves, whoosh—what a mess!
The vacuum laments its seasonal stress.
With pumpkins all grinning, we roast them in time,
Over snacks and stories, what a chaotic rhyme!

Winter flakes settle, quite light and so fluffy,
Mismatched mittens, they always look gruffy.
Hot cocoa spills and the marshmallows float,
Whimsical chaos in a cozy old coat.

## Dimensions of Desire

A closet of wishes, both big and quite small,
Found dreams and odd socks, oh where is my shawl?
Old magazines whisper of fashion replays,
As I find my past self in a curious haze.

A kitchen that's wild, like a culinary show,
Burnt toast and bold spices steal quite the flow.
Recipes laugh at my amateur flair,
As I concoct dishes that no one would dare.

The library teems with tomes stacked so high,
Each book's a portal, oh me, oh my!
Adventure awaits in a dust-covered spine,
Though it might just lead to a pint of wine.

Hallways stretch out, like a funhouse scene,
Where shadows play tricks and please intervene.
Every twist and turn, a riddle to tease,
In my home of oddities, I do as I please.

## Spaces for Solace

In the bathroom, a throne of solitary bliss,
With shampoo bottles and scents, I just can't miss.
Rubber ducks float in the bubbles galore,
Echoing laughter, oh, who could want more?

The living room's a patchwork of dreams and schemes,
With mismatched furniture, it's bursting at the seams.
Cushions conspire, they form a soft fort,
Where snuggles and stories create a sweet sport.

A porch swings gently, an entertainer's delight,
Where neighbors gossip till the fall of night.
Lemonade sips and cicadas chirp loud,
Here I find comfort, wrapped in my shroud.

But let's not forget the endless game of hide,
With so many nooks where silliness hides.
In each quirky space, my heart finds its song,
In these funny little rooms that all feel so wrong.

## Embracing Change

I painted my walls a shade of lime,
A color choice that felt sublime.
But friends just laughed, they couldn't take it,
Said they'd bring shades, I had to fake it.

The roof leaked on a sunny day,
My garden sprouted weeds at play.
I tried to fix, but made it worse,
My tools, I think, belong in a curse.

The kitchen's now a modern art,
With dishes stacked, a culinary heart.
I thought I'd bake a beautiful pie,
But smoke now billows like the sky.

In this wild ride of bumpy fun,
I've learned to laugh, I'm never done.
Change invites laughs, let's not complain,
In this silly place, I shall remain.

## Fragments of a Dreamscape

In dreamlands where the ceilings sing,
I lost my keys to everything.
The mattress floated, sweet as pie,
I jumped but landed on a butterfly.

My curtains danced like crazy waves,
And all my socks began to rave.
The fridge held secrets, tales to tell,
Of pizza parties, great and swell.

I painted floors with blue polka dots,
Declaring that it ties the knots.
But walking here's a tricky game,
Each step I take, it feels the same.

In this dreamscape, nothing's right,
Even the shadows giggle at night.
But here I thrive with whimsy's grace,
In my wild home of endless space.

## Corridors of a Forgotten Age

Wandering halls where echoes play,
With funny sounds that twist and sway.
The wallpaper laughs at tales once bold,
As dust bunnies gather stories untold.

A hallway stretch that leads to nowhere,
I find strange shoes and an old teddy bear.
The doors creak like they're sharing puns,
Each room holds memories and silly runs.

The attic's a circus, oh what a sight,
With cobwebs hanging, quite the delight.
The swing's a throne for dust-coated kings,
While mice in tuxedos play tiny strings.

So here I roam, what a surprise,
In forgotten ages, my laughter flies.
With every step through time and space,
I find the humor in this place.

## Portraits on the Walls

Portraits hang with faces odd,
One's a cat that looks like a god.
Next to a man in a floppy hat,
His grin is huge, his plans are flat.

A family of ducks quacks in glee,
Mocking my attempts to make tea.
The frames are crooked, just like my aim,
Yet somehow it feels like they're to blame.

Each picture tells a story weird,
Of pies that juggled, and cows that steered.
I laugh with each glance at that old frame,
Because in this chaos, it's all the same.

So here I dwell, with oddities bright,
In every portrait, a sparkling bite.
In laughter's warmth, I find my peace,
This whimsical gallery will never cease.

## Windows to the Soul

Glass panes that squeak,
Cats that like to peek,
A view of the street,
Where neighbors compete.

Dust bunnies play hide,
In the corners, they glide,
While I give a shout,
'Hey, get out, don't pout!'

Reflections of me,
Brushing crumbs from my knee,
Mirror chuckles bright,
When I dance with delight.

A smile in the frame,
Each glitch feels the same,
Behind those clear shields,
My laughter just yields.

## **Roofs of Resilience**

Tiles that wobble fast,
Weather never lasts,
But I laugh so loud,
Under storms unbowed.

Birds that make a nest,
Thinking this is best,
While I shake my head,
'You're not welcome, spread!'

The rain taps a beat,
A song that feels sweet,
Though leaks gift despair,
I just rock in my chair.

Breezes lift my sighs,
Beneath those vast skies,
With patches and smiles,
I conquer the miles.

## Shadows of Ancestors

Whispers in the halls,
Echo ancient calls,
With grumpy faced kin,
I laugh and dive in.

A ghost with a frown,
Tries to shake me down,
But I squeeze on past,
His gray chill won't last.

Footsteps made of fun,
Chasing shadows run,
In the chaos spun,
We dance 'til we're done.

Stories fill the room,
With laughter and gloom,
Each tale takes a turn,
In the fire, we burn.

## Hearthstone Heartbeats

Cracks in the flooring,
Let the critters in, alloring,
But as I chase mice,
I end up in a spice!

Pots that rattle loud,
Like some playful crowd,
Each boil is a song,
Where I often belong.

The kettle sings low,
As if putting on a show,
While friends gather near,
With snacks, lots of cheer.

Empty plates now tease,
'You'll clean us, if you please!'
Yet laughter rings bright,
Over meals every night.

## **Blossoms of Belonging**

In a place where socks disappear,
And old chairs come to cheer.
The fridge hums a silly tune,
While cats plot under the moon.

Each room has a quirky smell,
Like old shoes where treasures dwell.
Laughter echoes through the halls,
As light from a far window calls.

Sticky notes cover the door,
They remind us of the fun galore.
Dust bunnies hold an annual rave,
In the cozy nook where we misbehave.

A couch that's seen better days,
Wears cushions like it's on a phase.
With every creak, it shares a tale,
Of snacks we've dropped and pranks on scale.

## Portraits in Memory

Framed faces line the wall,
Some in shades, others small.
We giggle at the mismatched styles,
Captured in those old, goofy smiles.

The carpet's a maze of old stains,
Remnants of our wild campaigns.
A pizza slice from long ago,
Still has a story we all know.

The ceiling fan sways like a dancer,
While dust motes perform their jaunty prancer.
Every corner cradles our quirks,
In this stage where laughter lurks.

With echoes of childhood glee,
Every room is a memory spree.
And even though the paint may peel,
Fab stories linger like a hearty meal.

## **Seeds of Nostalgia**

In a garden where mishaps grow,
We planted dreams in rows and rows.
Each seedling's a mishmash of delight,
Sprouting mishaps that take flight.

The weeds, they dance like they know best,
While the flowers giggle in their jest.
Sunshine rains down, a silly sight,
As butterflies join in the light fight.

We harvested memories in a basket,
Twirling around like we're in a casket.
The fruits, they sing of days gone by,
Each one holds a childhood sigh.

In this plot where laughter blooms,
Our roots weave stories and dreams assume.
With every season, new joys sprout,
In this fun-filled garden, no doubt.

## An Odyssey of Structure

A fort made of blankets and dreams,
Where imagination bursts at the seams.
Wolf among sheep, with spoons as swords,
We venture out to foreign fjords.

With duct tape holding life together,
We dance like it's the best of weather.
Each creak of wood a call to arms,
As we defend our nightly charms.

The door squeaks like a rickety boat,
While logic takes a playful note.
Adventures spark in every nook,
As we scribble tales in our own book.

From paper-mâché to gleeful mess,
Our structure thrives on pure excess.
With giggles echoing down each lane,
We bask in chilly, sunny rain!

## Embrace of the Familiar

In my abode of quirky charm,
Each corner has a story, no harm.
The fridge hums a tune all night,
While socks dance like they've taken flight.

Chairs that creak like old grandmas,
Each scratch a memory, just because.
The cat rules the couch with flair,
While I just marvel at her golden hair.

Walls adorned with pictures askew,
Framed moments of joy, it's true.
With every laugh that fills the air,
I find my magic in this rare fair.

So here I stand, a merry host,
To memories that I cherish most.
Embracing chaos, I find my bliss,
At home, it's laughter sealed with a kiss.

## Axes of Affection

In a space where pillows collide,
I find joy and laughter inside.
With pizza boxes stacked so high,
I can't tell if I'm a chef or shy.

The bathroom's a jungle of hair ties,
A mirage of chaos, a sweet surprise.
The mirror speaks truths without refrain,
While toothpaste exploits my morning brain.

Friends flock here as if on cue,
For game nights filled with raucous 'who?'.
Their laughter echoes, a symphony bright,
Although they leave crumbs—what a sight!

And here we gather, in sweet disarray,
The axes of affection hold sway.
In every quirky cranny made,
Love is the joke we'll never trade.

## Spectrums of Space

In this lively realm of color and cheer,
The paint peels back my growing fear.
Each room a canvas, a raucous delight,
Filled with mismatched socks that spark joy at night.

The closet bursts with outfits bizarre,
You'd think it's a circus, and I'm the star.
Shoes mingle freely, a dance on the floor,
While jackets argue—who needs a door?

Sunlight spills in like grape juice spilled,
My windows are portals, my heart is thrilled.
I wave to the neighbors, they wave back in glee,
As I tumble through life in radical spree.

These zany spaces, peculiar and bright,
Stitch together warmth, an invisible light.
In the spectrum of chaos that makes my day,
I play with weirdness in every way.

## **Boundaries of Blessings**

Here we dwell within these walls,
Echoes of laughter, whimsy calls.
The carpet's stained with love and pie,
Each step a reminder, oh me, oh my!

Neighbors drop by with cookies rare,
While I hide my crumbs without a care.
Walls that wobble, flooring that creaks,
A home full of stories, quirks, and peaks.

Houseplants grin from their pots each day,
Their leafy laughter a merry play.
Dust bunnies throw a wild parade,
While we dance in shadows, unafraid.

These boundaries of blessings, snug and bright,
In a world that spins, we find our light.
With humor and love ever on display,
I count my blessings in a funny way.

## Echoing Laughter

In the yard, a chicken danced,
With silly socks, it pranced.
A goat with shades joined the spree,
Claiming it was born to be free.

The salad bowl wore a hat,
As cats debated, 'Who's fat?'
Goldfish giggled in their bowl,
Wishing for a stroll and a stroll.

The mailbox tried to sing a tune,
But only spat out last month's moon.
Windows winked to folks outside,
'Join our party!' they chimed with pride.

Through the walls, the echoes fly,
Laughter bounces way up high.
As I wonder what is real,
In this place, I love to squeal.

## **Nestled in Dreams**

Pillows stacked like little forts,
Where skunks wear ruffled shorts.
The blanket's a dragon, fierce and bold,
With stories of treasure and secrets untold.

Nightlights twinkle like stars at play,
To monsters' smiles at the end of the day.
A closet full of giggles and schemes,
Hiding clothes that smell like dreams.

The bed's a ship on a sea of thoughts,
Where socks are pirates, all tangled knots.
In slumber's grasp, humor unfolds,
As snoring echoes, the mystery holds.

Awake in the morning, I rise with flair,
Thankful for wonders hidden everywhere.
In this haven, where silliness beams,
Life's a tapestry woven with dreams.

## The Architecture of Affection

A coffee cup glued to the chair,
While socks form a bridge for the cat who dares.
Chairs debate with the table's pride,
While crumbs hold meetings—what a wild ride!

The fridge hums tunes from days of old,
Eggs cracking jokes, feeling bold.
In the oven, cookies plot and scheme,
Whispering secrets of a sugary dream.

Walls painted with laughter and fun,
Each tickle of sunlight, a race to run.
Feelings shaped like cupcakes and pies,
In this quirky joint, joy never lies.

With laughter as the beams that hold,
Our silly structure, a sight to behold.
Love built strong on this playful ground,
In every corner, a blessing found.

## Passageways of Time

Through the hallway, echoes prance,
Ghosts of socks in a joyful dance.
The clock spins tales of tickle fights,
While dust bunnies chase the starlit lights.

Stairs that creak a tune so sweet,
As shoes tango on tiny feet.
Hallway photos wink and grin,
Capturing mischief, where stories begin.

Behind each door, a treasure waits,
You might find a cake or two plates.
In corners, stories curl and twist,
Chronicles of the things we've missed.

Time slips by with laughter's embrace,
In this passageway, we find our place.
Each moment a melody, light and chime,
Celebrating our journey through whimsical time.

## **Homeward Reflections**

I hung a picture crooked, a crooked smile,
While searching for my keys, I laughed all the while.
My cat is the ruler, my dog thinks he's king,
In this lively circus, oh what joy they'll bring.

With socks that don't match, I dance through the halls,
Echoes of laughter are my favorite calls.
The fridge hums a tune, like a party gone wrong,
Every day's an adventure, where chaos belongs.

The broom and I tango, we twirl and we spin,
No one said cleaning was a sinful grin.
Dust bunnies fly, like they're part of the show,
In this quirky kingdom, we always steal the glow.

So here's to my castle, both crazy and bright,
Laughter is king, and the chaos feels right.
With echoes of joy and a sprinkle of cheer,
Each reflection is home, for it's laughter we steer.

## The Legacy of Stone

In a fortress of whimsy with walls made of cheese,
My plans constructed swiftly, but please mind the bees.
The garden's a jungle, where gnomes rise and bow,
A legacy laid down by me and my cow.

The roof's built of pancakes that sizzle and flip,
My neighbors all chuckle, they say it's a trip.
When rain showers fall, syrup cascades down,
Drenched in laughter, I wear a syrup crown.

Foundations of marshmallow, though fragile and sweet,
Crack under the weight of a bold dancing feat.
We carve out our dreams on this soft, gooey land,
With a funny bonanza, life's perfectly planned.

So let's toast to this silliness, walls made of fun,
A legacy forged with a pun and a pun.
In a world made of whimsy, I reign as king,
With laughter as armor, let the joy bells ring.

## Fables in the Foyer

In the foyer of stories, where tales take a spin,
A squirrel stole my keys and darted back in.
The shoes by the door tell the stories they've lived,
In this vibrant entrance, oh how much joy's given.

With hats on the ceiling, an umbrella or two,
My foyer's a circus, that's vibrant and new.
The dust bunnies gather, they gossip and cheer,
While I trip on a toy, with laughter so near.

A console of quirks, with buttons that gleam,
Every visit feels like stepping into a dream.
So bring on the stories, the silliness bold,
In my foyer of fables, let the laughter unfold.

Wipe your shoes at the door, don't mind if you stray,
In the land of the funny, come join in the play.
With whimsical wonders and giggles galore,
Each step in this foyer opens up a new floor.

## Memories Beneath the Shingles

Beneath the shingles, where the shadows peek,
A treasure trove of memories, unique yet antique.
With laughter contained in a jar on the shelf,
The moments we cherish, we keep for ourselves.

The attic's a kingdom of rust and of dust,
Where forgotten toys giggle, it's a must.
A pet rock and a rubber band, guardians of time,
In the humor of days, we dance and we rhyme.

This roof keeps our secrets, our giggles intact,
While a stray spider spins tales that we've never lacked.
Our stories are woven in the beams of this space,
With the remnants of laughter, let joy interlace.

So here's to the memories that tickle and gleam,
Beneath funny shingles where we laugh and we dream.
Each knock on the beam, every creak of the floor,
In this house of laughter, we always want more.

## Navigating the Familiar

In the hallway, I trip on a shoe,
A ghost of my youth, it seems all too true.
Each corner I turn, I meet my old cat,
Who yells like a neighbor, 'You can't have my mat!'

The fridge has declared, 'It's time to eat chips!'
But no one advised of the crunching loud flips.
The chair creaks a tune, a rickety song,
While I wonder how long it can hold me along.

## A Nest of Nurture

The couch has a dent, it knows my shape well,
It hugs me at night like a cushy hotel.
Pillows are strewn like confetti in air,
A nest of my clutter, with love and a chair.

The kitchen's a circus, with pots on parade,
While I mastermind meals with a spatula blade.
Spices collude, while I taste-test a pinch,
Who knew basil could rival my Uncle's old quinch?

## Hearthstones and Heartstrings

The fireplace groans, it's been years since it burned,
Yet I shovel in logs, though it never quite learned.
Like old friends around, they remind me of cheer,
But all we get now is a tickle, not here.

Cookies are baking, the smell wafts around,
With flour on my nose, I look foolish, unbound.
The smoke alarm shouts, a cacophony loud,
While I wave like a nut in an ill-prepared crowd.

## Pillars of Tradition

Grandma's old chair is now a display,
With cat hair and dust, the memories stay.
It squeaks and it squeals, a ghostly duet,
Of family stories I'll never forget.

The holiday lights are a riotous mess,
Each year I untangle, I can only guess.
They twinkle with joy, or maybe they frown,
Saying 'Here we go, let's light up the town!'

## A Hearth of Warm Debates

In the kitchen, we gather round,
Where laughter is the sweetest sound.
Chairs squeak as the opinions fly,
Honey, you're wrong—just let it die!

The dog steals the last slice of pie,
And everyone lets out a sigh.
Arguments over who's the best cook,
While secretly peeking at each recipe book.

My uncle claims he's quite the chef,
Yet the smoke alarm has lost its breath.
We laugh as the dinner burns to ash,
This meal? Oh well, just a quick dash.

Yet here in chaos, love persists,
In every laugh, we find our bliss.
Though dishes pile up high and wide,
In this warm bickering, we take pride.

## The Blueprint of My Heart

With crayons drawn on a napkin sheet,
I sketched my dreams, oh what a feat!
A living room, or maybe two,
A pool that's filled with soda, too.

My plans were grand, a perfect maze,
Yet the floors all tilted in strange ways.
Doors that lead to nowhere fast,
Was that the plan? I'm sure it passed.

I put a garden in the hall,
For veggies tall, but they were small.
I water them with hopes and dreams,
Yet all I got were slimy greens.

But still I chuckle, what a sight,
Each strange design brings pure delight.
In every corner, a quirky part,
A goofy laugh, the blueprint of my heart.

## Gathering Dust and Memories

In corners hide the toys of yore,
Covered in dust, they beg for war.
Time forgot their noble quests,
Now silent soldiers in their vests.

Each shelf a tale of forgotten days,
Full of laughter, chaos, and wild plays.
This tricycle, once a speedster bike,
Now just a relic, oh what a hike!

I dust them off, let memories flow,
Like ancient soldiers in a show.
"Oh look, there's my cape from '93!"
Fighting villains in my own reality.

Yet here they sit, all out of sight,
Waiting for kids to reignite.
In every rusted, dusty nook,
Are laughter's echoes, my favorite book.

## **Framed by Time**

In frames of wood and crooked lines,
Memories hang like funny signs.
A holiday where Uncle Stan
Wore tinsel like it was the plan.

Snapshots of moments gone awry,
Like Grandma's dance that made us cry.
Every picture tells a jest,
Of family fun, we're truly blessed.

Time ticks on, but we just laugh,
At Dad's new haircut, a little daft.
Each detail captured, funny and grand,
These painted memories, life unplanned.

So here we are, a quirky crew,
In frames adorned, with tales anew.
In every glance, a chuckle chimes,
Together framed, we dance through times.

## The Dance of Shadows

In the corner, a cat takes the lead,
While the broom waltzes, oh what a deed!
Dust bunnies twirl, with a giggle and cheer,
Even the cobwebs seem to disappear.

A lamp starts to sway, with a flickering light,
Chairs join the party, they spin left and right.
The fridge hums a tune, what a sight to behold,
As leftovers jive to the rhythm so bold.

Windows peek in, they're part of the fun,
Casting shadows that dance in the sun.
Laughter erupts from the walls with delight,
A gathering of joy, oh what a night!

But wait—who's that? An intruder is near,
The mischievous squirrel, oh dear, oh dear!
He's here for a snack, not a step on the floor,
Join the dance, friend, then we'll open the door!

## Sanctuary of Whispers

Whispers of secrets in every thin wall,
Echoes of laughter, they bounce like a ball.
The fridge shares a tale of an old pot roast,
While the plants spill gossip amongst themselves most.

The creaky old floorboards, they squeak with glee,
As the curtains debate who's the fairest to see.
The carpet replays every footstep of doubt,
But the ceiling light grins, knowing what it's about.

Socks have gone missing, not one can be found,
Into the abyss, they swirl all around.
But the couch keeps it cozy with cushions so plump,
Saying, "Take a seat, let's gather the lump!"

A sanctuary built of chatter and cheer,
Where every crevice holds stories so dear.
In this abode where hilarity lives,
Even the tick-tock of time sometimes gives!

## The Heartbeat of a Dwelling

The tick-tock of time keeps the rhythm alive,
Walls start to whisper, oh how they thrive!
A heart beats within, made of wood and of stone,
With laughter and mishaps, it's never alone.

The oven hums softly, a warm friend it stays,
While the sink chuckles gently, rinsing the craze.
Spatulas dance on the counter, oh boy,
As pots join in with a clang and a ploy!

A window flutters like a winged delight,
Opening wide to the stars at night.
Neighbors peek through, with a grin and a jest,
"Is that your cat, or are you just blessed?"

In this funny heart, where chaos does dwell,
Lives a laughter that sticks, like a sweet caramel.
Every nook is a friend, every cranny a muse,
In this lively abode, you can't really lose!

## Chronicles of Comfort

Once there was a couch that had seen better days,
With cushions all lumpy, and stories to praise.
It cradled the family with saggy embrace,
While popcorn confessions filled every small space.

The TV remote, like a knight on its quest,
Fought battles of boredom, it gave its best jest.
Together they conquered the shows of the night,
As the snacks rang the bell for a glorious bite!

A closet once packed, now a jungle to roam,
Unleashing forgotten treasures from home.
The socks in the back throw a wild little bash,
While the coats try to tango, a colorful clash!

So grab a warm blanket, let's cozy it up,
With giggles and stories, we'll drink from the cup.
In chronicles written where laughter is king,
This sanctuary blooms—oh, the joy it can bring!

## **Secrets Behind Closed Doors**

In the attic, dust bunnies reign,
While the cat thinks it's a game.
Socks go missing, under the bed,
Like secrets that remain unsaid.

The fridge hums its midnight tune,
As leftovers plot under the moon.
Whispers echo from the floor,
What will they find behind the door?

Mismatched chairs tell tales of woe,
Of family feasts in an epic show.
The couch, a throne for all to see,
Holds treasures hidden, just for me.

So passersby may think it's quaint,
But inside lurks a cat who's faint.
With toys and treats all piled high,
It's a circus, not a secure sky!

## Stories Woven in Wood

The floorboards creak like old folks do,
Sharing gossip 'bout me and you.
Each scratch and dent, a story told,
Of hearts lost, and treasures bold.

The shelves sigh with books stacked tight,
Of knights in shining, paper-light.
But beware the one that's askew,
For it might just bear a ghostly view!

Wobbly tables hold drinks with flair,
When guests arrive, they take their chair.
"My drink's too strong!" a friend may yell,
But it's just the wood holding its spell!

In this fortress of timber dreams,
Squirrels dance and sunlight beams.
So here's to laughter, stories, and quirk,
In this woodwork where smiles lurk!

## A Sanctuary of Sunlight

Sunshine spills across the floor,
Chasing shadows out the door.
Dust motes dancing in the rays,
While the dog snores through the days.

Curtains flutter like a sail,
As the breeze tells a windy tale.
A chair in the sun, my favorite spot,
Where time stands still, but my tea is hot!

Laughter rings from the garden fair,
While sibling squabbles fill the air.
'Don't touch my toy!' the youngest screams,
As they plot a takeover of sunny dreams.

A sanctuary where giggles bloom,
And every room holds its own loom.
Weaving joy like threads of light,
In the warmth of this sunny delight!

## The Threshold of New Beginnings

With each knock, the door swings wide,
Uninvited guests take a ride.
A cat springs forth, in a show of glee,
'Welcome to chaos! Come and see!'

Old shoes line the entryway,
Each with stories, come what may.
Had a good life, now they stand,
While memories linger, hand-in-hand.

Call it a threshold, if you dare,
For life races by like it's a fair.
One day bloom, the next, a mess,
With laughter hiding the slight excess!

So here we stand, in laughter's thrall,
One step inside, you'll feel it all.
A place for mischief, joy, and jest,
Where every moment is truly blessed!

## Tales of Timelessness

In the corner sat a chair,
With a cushion quite askew.
The cat claimed it as her throne,
Where she plotted her next mew.

The bathroom door, it squeaks and creaks,
Like it's got a tale to tell.
With every step, the floorboards groan,
As if they're under a spell.

The kitchen's always full of crumbs,
From cereal left out too long.
The fridge hums a silly song,
While dodging spills—it feels so wrong.

And in the garden, gnomes stand still,
With silly grins they just can't hide.
They watch the squirrels steal the show,
As acorns tumble, oh what a ride!

## Imprints of Innocence

There's a big mark on the wall,
A height chart of little feet.
A clumsy climb, a joyous fall,
Memories rich and oh so sweet.

The crayons colored in wild ways,
On tabletops and every chair.
"Is it art?" the guests all say,
While parents just breathe a prayer.

A jelly stain hugs the floor,
A vibrant carpet surprise.
As sticky fingers reach for more,
It's dessert that wins the prize!

Lego towers scrape the sky,
Each brick a battle won with flair.
With giggles echoing nearby,
Childhood magic fills the air.

## **Nestled in Dreams**

Beneath the quilt, a secret land,
Where socks have vanished, no one knows.
The pillows form a wonder band,
Late-night giggles freely flow.

The closet's home to silly beasts,
Who wear the clothes of yesterday.
In dreams, they host rambunctious feasts,
When bedtime throws the light away.

A stuffed giraffe keeps watchful eyes,
Over adventures yet to bloom.
Each nighttime whisper softly sighs,
As stars spill light within the room.

With blankets piled like snowy hills,
The moon plays peekaboo at night.
In this realm of dreams and thrills,
Everything's softer, oh so bright!

## Shelves of Stories

On the shelves, a jungle grows,
Where books compete for every space.
With covers wild and tales that glow,
Each spine a spark of joy and grace.

The volumes chat, the novels squabble,
As dust motes dance in sunlit beams.
A world crafted from written rubble,
Where every page has hidden dreams.

A pile of tales, precarious,
One wrong nudge, disaster waits.
Each time I read, I'm curious,
Hoping dog-eared lore relates!

From mysteries to fables bright,
Adventure calls from every shelf.
Where literacy takes flight,
And laughter's found within oneself.

## Tapestry of Family

In a kitchen bustling with cheer,
Grandma's recipes always near.
Dad trips over his own two feet,
The sight is surely a funny treat.

Sister sings off-key, such delight,
While the dog barks, joining the fight.
Cats play king on the couch's reign,
This symphony drives me quite insane.

Uncle's jokes fall flat, what a blast,
Yet the laughter echoes, unsurpassed.
Mom rolls her eyes, but can't resist,
In this chaos, we coexist.

Family portraits, we can't agree,
Did we all wear those socks for free?
Yet love weaves through us, thicker than glue,
In this tapestry, we laugh, we grew.

## Rooms Painted in Light

In the living room, socks on the wall,
It's a gallery of chaos, that's our call.
Lampshades askew, a colorful sight,
Each corner alive, with laughter and light.

The kitchen's the hub, where we all stray,
Dinner seems miles but we eat anyway.
Spills and thrills while we dance and twirl,
The fridge hums along, our culinary whirl.

In the hallway, echoes from a stray cat,
Chasing the dust bunnies—not where it's at!
But the giggles remind us to hold tight,
These rooms are our joy, painted in light.

Bathroom antics and squeaky-clean scenes,
Adventures unfold like daily routines.
Mirror reflections, who looks the best?
We laugh at our hair—and ignore the rest.

## Shelters of Solitude

In my corner, a fortress of pillows,
I plot my escape from the loud, wild willows.
A blanket fort's built, no grown-ups allowed,
Here, I reign supreme; I'm quiet and proud.

Socks as my warriors, stuffed bears in line,
Together we conquer, oh, isn't it fine?
Yet, every so often, I need a reprieve,
From chatter and chaos, I happily leave.

The bathroom's a haven, or so I declare,
With bubbles and books—only peace in there!
Mom shouts my name; I stay silent, intent,
Shelters of solitude, my time well spent.

But then a cat jumps, and I let out a squeal,
Crash goes the fortress—what a raw deal!
My kingdom now crumbles, the battle is lost,
Yet laughter erupts, no matter the cost.

## **Retreats of Reflection**

In the nook by the window, I hide with a grump,
Staring at clouds, feeling quite like a chump.
But oh! Look at that one, it looks like a shoe!
Giggles escape, and my mood starts anew.

Chasing the sunbeams that dance on the floor,
Each one an adventure, knocking at the door.
Reflections of laughter peel back every doubt,
Even my shadow is joining the shout.

The silence is stirr'd by a comic parade,
As squirrels create a hilarious charade.
They're plotting and planning, or so it seems,
While I sit and ponder my wild, wacky dreams.

Oh, these retreats offer more than they lack,
A moment of stillness from all the loud clack.
With humor unbound, I stand up with flair,
Reflecting on life, and I simply don't care.

## **Cedars of Comfort**

In my backyard, I've got some trees,
A crooked fence, and buzzing bees.
The posts are leaning, quite a sight,
Still, we hold barbecues every night.

The roof's slightly sagging, and that's okay,
It adds character, like my pop's toupee.
Squirrels play tag, up and down,
While we sip lemonade, looking like a clown.

The door creaks open with a quirky squeal,
It's our welcome mat, it's got some appeal.
Neighbors smile with curious glances,
Wondering how we manage our home romances.

Laughter echoes through the halls,
As my kids make forts out of old sheets and walls.
Life's a circus with popcorn and cheer,
In this quirky joint, I hold dear.

## Embers of Homecoming

As I enter, I trip on a shoe,
Maybe my life's a comedy too.
The oven's hot, must check the pie,
Hope it's not burnt, or I'll just cry.

The chairs are mismatched, but who cares?
They add flavor, like strawberries in pairs.
Friends gather 'round, we laugh and tease,
With stories of failings and heights to appease.

The cat's on the counter, looking all proud,
As if she's hosting a fancy crowd.
Chasing the dog, they make quite the scene,
In this funny place, between circus and serene.

Each time we return, there's love in the air,
Even when socks go missing, it's rare.
Memories light like embers aglow,
In this joyful chaos, we all grow.

## Stepping Stones of Growth

My sidewalk's lumpy, a gravel delight,
With cracks big enough to start a fight.
Grass grows wild, like it's lost in a race,
Wandering around without a trace.

Garden gnomes with silly grins,
Watch as I stumble, waiting to win.
In this place, I learn and fall,
Each stone a lesson, oh, what a ball!

The fence is paint-chipped, but so full of cheer,
A landmark of laughter, held so dear.
Here we grow up, and sometimes down,
Wearing our triumphs like a crown.

With friends and family, we tread these paths,
Making memories, igniting our laughs.
Through stormy weathers and sunny rays,
This crazy journey forever stays.

## Serenity in Structures

In this space, nothing is straight,
Walls lean in a slightly odd state.
Windows open with a creak and a groan,
As laughter erupts, filling our home.

The ceiling's low, but spirits are high,
Under fear of bumping, we give it a try.
Oops! I hit my head, what a surprise,
It's like a low-budget, cheeky reprise.

Decor's a mix of colors galore,
From grandma's quilt to that old surfboard.
Each frame tells a tale, some fuzzy, some clear,
This playful chaos is blissfully near.

As we gather 'round for the evening meal,
With stories and laughter, that's our appeal.
Finding peace in the awkward and funny,
In this wild structure, we say it's all sunny.

## A Canvas of Laughter

I hung up my socks on the laundry line,
They waved like flags, looking quite divine.
The curtains are mismatched, a vibrant spree,
Like a clown's bowtie, just waiting for tea.

I painted the walls in a bubblegum hue,
Each stroke a giggle, every splash anew.
My cat wears a crown, oh what a scene,
Queen of the castle, she reigns like a dream.

The floors creak and groan, they seem to dance,
With every footstep, they sway and prance.
I've got a fridge that hums a sweet tune,
Whispering secrets under the shiny moon.

So come for a visit, bring snacks and cheer,
This place is a circus, but laughter is near.
With joy on the shelves and smiles all around,
In this quirky abode, pure humor is found.

## Echoes of Yesterday

The attic's a treasure, a quirky delight,
With old toys and dolls, they giggle at night.
I found my old bike, a three-wheeled beast,
Painted like rainbows, it calls for a feast.

In corners, old shoes, mismatched for fun,
Each pair tells a tale, oh, the races we run.
The walls whisper stories of mishaps and glee,
Of birthdays and blunders, wild as can be.

The photo frames wobble, a sight to behold,
Stretched smiles and grins, with stories retold.
Here's me in a tutu, my brother in sneakers,
A shocking resemblance—both laughing behind speakers.

So let's raise a glass to the past we hold dear,
To echoes of laughter that never disappear.
With memories wrapped in a zany embrace,
In this wonderful chaos, we've found our place.

## The Roof of Resilience

The shingles are crooked, a sight to see,
With patches of clouds, they giggle with glee.
In rainstorms, they dance, like a lively crew,
Beating drums of water, a musical view.

A satellite dish with a tinfoil hat,
Catching the gossip, where's the next chat?
My chimney's a whistle, it sings with the breeze,
A tune for the birds and a call to the bees.

It sways with the seasons, resilient and bold,
With jokes for the sun and some stories retold.
Oh, storms may come, but with laughter we stand,
This roof's like a party, we dance hand in hand.

So let's toast to the top, where the fun never ends,
With laughter as shelter and joy as our friends.
In this quirky abode, we make our own way,
Each moment a memory, come laugh, come play!

## Windows to My Soul

My windows are wide, with stickers galore,
A sneaky raccoon peeks in from the floor.
With wavy glass panes like a funhouse mirror,
The world looks so silly, the view couldn't be clearer.

They catch rainbows and giggles that float on by,
With each passing cloud, painted smiles in the sky.
Each window's a stage with a curious play,
The birds act the part, coming out every day.

I've got one that squeaks, it's a musical gem,
When it opens wide, it sings just for them.
Neighbors stop by for a laugh or a wink,
With sunlight as stage lights, we dance and we think.

So come peek inside, take a look, take a chance,
Let laughter pour in, join this joyous dance.
These windows are portals, a smile all around,
In the heart of the chaos, pure humor is found.

## **Rooms of Reminiscence**

In the kitchen, spills and thrills,
A dance of pots and clanking grills.
The fridge hums tunes of late-night snacks,
Where leftovers conspire, no need for racks.

The living room, a throne of fluff,
Where cats hold court, they strut and bluff.
Remote controls lost in the couch abyss,
As laughter echoes in playful bliss.

In the bathroom, a rubber duck parade,
Suds and giggles in the escapade.
Mirror selfies with silly faces,
This room's the king of all funny places.

Finally, the attic holds secrets untold,
Dusty treasures and memories bold.
A clown costume from a distant past,
In this space, the fun never lasts!

## A Sanctuary of Stories

A reading nook draped in sunlight's glow,
Where books come alive, and wild tales flow.
A cat on my lap, giving me sighs,
While I chuckle at where the hero flies.

In the dining room, a food fight ensues,
Flying spaghetti and forbidden stews.
Grandma's old recipes sprout wings of flair,
Each meal's a battle, oh what a scare!

The hallway's a gallery of faces absurd,
With portraits skewed and laughter heard.
Family snapshots, oh what a mess,
A treasure of quirks, I must confess.

The garden blooms with laughter's delight,
As gnomes dance under the moonlit night.
Where veggies giggle and flowers wink,
In this whimsical place, I pause to think.

## The Heartbeat of Home

In the heart of the home, a symphony plays,
Chairs creak and squeak in their funny ways.
The dog steals socks, a mischievous thief,
Each room's a chapter of comedic grief.

Laughter spills like coffee in the hall,
From jokes misplaced, and wonders small.
The stairs are a slide, it's all in the fun,
Every wrong step's a race just begun.

The pantry's a trap for the silly sweet,
Cookie jars bursting with crumbs at my feet.
Each munch becomes a giggling spree,
In this quirky realm, we're wild and free.

The backyard's a stage for antics bright,
With neighbors watching, our clowns take flight.
Sprinklers pop like silent popcorn,
In this lively place where laughs are worn.

## **Crafted Corners**

In the corner, a chair with a spindly leg,
Leans precarious like a three-legged beg.
Every creak a story; every wobble a tale,
Of moments gone by that never grow stale.

Underneath the stairs, a shoe box lid,
Holds treasures forgotten, no child would rid.
Old birthday cards and a rubber band,
In this realm of joy, things are quite grand.

The porch swing sways in its rhythmic charm,
Where stories are told, and we feel the warmth.
Neighbors gather, as gossip takes flight,
In this lovely ambience, all feels right.

The corner of the garage, a kingdom of junk,
Where treasures await if you give them a thunk.
This cluttered nook holds joys yet to find,
In every crafted corner, laughter's entwined.

**Spaces for New Beginnings**

In a spot where clutters clash,
I find a place to make it splash.
With mismatched chairs and colors bright,
My chaos shines, a pure delight.

A table made of wonky wood,
My friends laugh hard, it feels so good.
The creaky floor sings out a tune,
We dance like loons beneath the moon.

A fridge that hums a silly song,
Its strange aroma won't be long.
We munch on snacks, then start to scheme,
Inventing dreams like a wild team.

So here's to spaces full of grin,
Where laughter echoes deep within.
Each corner tells a joke or two,
With memories bright, and friendships true.

## The Tapestry of Togetherness

In the corners where the dust bunnies play,
We tell stories that stretch night to day.
With mismatched socks and scattered shoes,
We spin tales that tickle and amuse.

A couch that swallows when you sit,
Offers comfort, though it may not fit.
We dump our bags like weary gnomes,
And find our comfort in these homes.

A dining table that's always spread,
With crumbs and laughter, we're well-fed.
We may not have fine china or flair,
But every meal is a treasure to share.

So here's to bonds that never break,
In this fantastic, quirky landscape.
A tapestry of love and laughter,
Woven tight, happily ever after.

## Breath of the Framework

With beams enlisted in a quirky fight,
Our framework sways, but feels just right.
Walls may wobble as we shimmy around,
Each creak and groan is a joyful sound.

In this wild parade of clashing colors,
We find our peace, despite some blunders.
Windows framed by plants gone wild,
Reflect our joy, quirky and mild.

The roof above may have a leak,
Yet underneath, we all still speak.
We gather close for games and fun,
Around a table, we've just begun.

With laughter echoing through the air,
We find our joys, a treasure rare.
In the structure of laughter, we intertwine,
A hodgepodge life, goofy and divine.

## **Whispers Beneath the Roof**

Underneath the whimsical roof,
Whispers of mischief dance aloof.
We play hide-and-seek in the hallway's bend,
Laughing like kids, never want it to end.

Each room a stage for laughter so bright,
Where shadows play and dreams ignite.
With quirks and quibbles, we navigate,
Finding joy in the little things we celebrate.

From the attic filled with old, odd stuff,
To the basement where the echoes puff.
We share secrets like they're our own,
In this crazy place we've called home.

So here's to giggles and silly scoffs,
To rickety chairs and playful scoffs.
In this abode where laughter lives,
We gather close, and the heart gives.

www.ingramcontent.com/pod-product-compliance
Lightning Source LLC
Chambersburg PA
CBHW060115230426
43661CB00003B/189